The Conflict Management Skills Workbook

Self-Assessments, Exercises
& Educational Handouts

Ester A. Leutenberg

John J. Liptak, EdD

Illustrated by

Amy L. Brodsky, LISW-S

wholeperson
Stress & Wellness Publishers
Duluth, Minnesota

Whole Person Associates

101 W. 2nd St., Suite 203
Duluth, MN 55802

800-247-6789

books@wholeperson.com
www.wholeperson.com

The Conflict Management Skills Workbook
Self-Assessments, Exercises & Educational Handouts

Printed in the United States of America

10 9 8 7 6 5 4 3 2 1

Editorial Director: Carlene Sippola
Art Director: Joy Morgan Dey

Library of Congress Control Number: 2010926457
ISBN: 978-1-57025-239-6

Using This Book *(For the professional)*

In many ways, conflict is a basic fact of life. We have all experienced conflict in our personal and professional lives. Because conflicts are disagreements resulting from people or groups having differences in attitudes, beliefs, values or needs, there will be times when conflict is inevitable. People experience differences in any relationship. That conflict exists is not a bad situation, as long as the conflict is managed effectively. Resolving conflicts can be beneficial and lead to growth and maturity. Outcomes of constructive conflict management will increase confidence in several aspects of life management:

- awareness that problems exist and need to be solved
- creative problem solving and decision making
- sense of well-being
- motivation and energy to take action
- implications / attitudes / responses of empathy and caring
- commitment to relationships
- impact of respect, trust and commitment

Any conflict has the potential to be incredibly destructive to a relationship. Managed in the wrong way, it can lead to extreme differences between people that can quickly spiral out of control. Each person will experience this Negotiations Model based on their point of view in a conflict as they use the following format to help them resolve their issues / problems:

NEGOTIATIONS MODEL

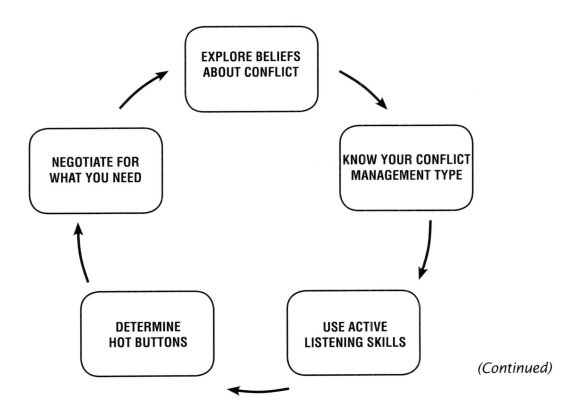

(Continued)

Using This Book *(For the professional, continued)*

The Conflict Management Skills Workbook contains five separate sections to help participants learn more about themselves and the skills they possess to manage conflicts that occur in their lives. Participants will learn new skills and their importance in preventing and resolving conflicts.

The sections are:

1) **BELIEFS ABOUT CONFLICT SCALE** helps individuals to explore their beliefs about the process and outcomes of conflicts.

2) **CONFLICT MANAGEMENT STYLES SCALE** helps individuals identify their preferred style for managing conflict.

3) **LISTENING FOR MEANING SCALE** helps individuals to examine the active listening skills they possess for preventing conflicts and then dealing with conflict situations.

4) **HOT BUTTONS SCALE** helps individuals identify the situations that trigger conflict in their lives.

6) **NEGOTIATION STYLE SCALE** helps individuals identify their negotiation style for what they want and need.

Each section serves as an avenue for individual self-reflection, as well as for group experiences revolving around identified topics of importance. Each assessment includes directions for easy administration, scoring and interpretation. Also included are exploratory activities, reflective journaling activities and educational handouts to help participants discover their habitual effective and ineffective conflict management skills. Finally, instruction is provided for enhancing participants most critical weaknesses when attempting to prevent or resolve real-life conflicts.

 The art of self-reflection goes back many centuries and is rooted in many of the world's greatest spiritual and philosophical traditions. Socrates, the ancient Greek philosopher, was known to walk the streets engaging the people he met in philosophical reflection and dialogue. He felt that this type of activity was so important in life that he went so far as to proclaim, "The unexamined life is not worth living!" The unexamined life is one in which the same routine is continually repeated without ever thinking about its meaning to one's life and how one's life really could be lived. However, a structured reflection and examination of beliefs, assumptions, characteristics and patterns can provide a better understanding, which can lead to a more satisfying life. A greater level of self-understanding about important life skills is often necessary to make positive, self-directed changes in the negative patterns that keep repeating. The assessments and exercises in this book can help promote this self-understanding. Through involvement in the in-depth activities, participants claim ownership in the development of positive patterns.

(Continued)

Using This Book *(For the professional, continued)*

Journaling is an extremely powerful tool for enhancing self-discovery, learning, transcending traditional problems, breaking ineffective life habits, and helping to heal from psychological traumas of the past. From a physical point of view, writing reduces stress and lowers muscle tension, blood pressure and heart rate levels. Psychologically, writing reduces sadness, depression and general anxiety, and leads to a greater level of life satisfaction and optimism. Behaviorally, writing leads to enhanced social skills, emotional intelligence and creativity. It also leads to improved relationships through being able to effectively manage conflicts that occur in professional and personal relationships.

By combining reflective assessment and journaling, participants will be exposed to a powerful method of combining verbalizing and writing to reflect on and solve problems. Participants will become more aware of the strength and weaknesses of their specific conflict management and negotiation skills.

Preparation for using the assessments and activities in this book is important. The authors suggest that prior to administering any of the assessments in this book, you complete them yourself. This will familiarize you with the format of the assessments, the scoring directions, the interpretation guides and the journaling activities. Although the assessments are designed to be self-administered, scored and interpreted, this familiarity will help prepare facilitators to answer questions about the assessments for participants.

The Assessments, Journaling Activities, and Educational Handouts

The Assessments, Journaling Activities, and Educational Handouts in *The Conflict Management Skills Workbook* are reproducible and ready to be photocopied for participants' use. Assessments contained in this book focus on self-reported data and are similar to ones used by psychologists, counselors, and therapists. The accuracy and usefulness of the information provided is dependent on the truthful information that each participant provides through self-examination. By being honest, participants help themselves to learn about their hot buttons that cause conflicts with other people, their style of handling conflicts, and the skills needed to effectively handle, or even prevent, conflicts.

An assessment instrument can provide participants with valuable information about themselves; however, it cannot measure or identify everything about them. The purposes of the assessments are not to pigeon-hole certain characteristics, but rather to allow participants to explore all of their characteristics. This book contains self-assessments, not tests. Tests measure knowledge or whether something is right or wrong. For the assessments in this book, there are no right or wrong answers. These assessments ask for personal opinions or attitudes about a topic of importance in the participant's life.

When administering the assessments in this workbook, remember that although the items are generically written so that they will be applicable to a wide variety of people, they will not account for every possible variable for every person. Use the assessments to help participants identify possible negative themes in their lives and find ways to break the hold of these patterns and their effects.

Advise the participants taking the assessments that they should not spend too much time trying to analyze the content of the questions; their initial response will most likely be true. Regardless of individual scores, encourage participants to talk about their findings and their feelings pertaining to what they have discovered about themselves. Talking about health, wellness, and overall well-being as it relates to conflict can enhance the life of participants. These wellness exercises can be used by group facilitators working with any populations who want to strengthen their overall wellness.

A particular score on any assessment does not guarantee a participant's level of conflict management skill. Use discretion when using any of the information or feedback provided in this workbook. The use of these assessments should not be substituted for consultation and/or counseling from a psychological or medical professional.

Thanks to the following professionals whose input in this book has been invaluable!

Kathy Khalsa, MAJS, OTR/L

Jay Leutenberg

Kathy Liptak, Ed.D.

Eileen Regen, M.Ed., CJE

Lucy Ritzic, OTR/L

Betty Welch, Ph.D.

Layout of the Book

This book includes the following reproducibles in all 5 sections:

- **Assessment Instruments** – Self-assessment inventories with scoring directions and interpretation materials. Group facilitators can choose one or more of the activities relevant to their participants.
- **Activity Handouts** – Practical questions and activities that prompt self-reflection and promote self-understanding. These questions and activities foster introspection and promote pro-social behaviors.
- **Reflective Questions for Journaling** – Self-exploration activities and journaling exercises specific to each assessment to enhance self-discovery, learning, and healing.
- **Educational Handouts** – Handouts designed to supplement instruction can be used individually or in groups. They can be distributed, converted into masters for overheads or transparencies, scanned or transferred to PowerPoint slides for use with LCD projectors, or written on a display for discussion.

Who should use this program?

This book has been designed as a practical tool for helping professional therapists, counselors, marriage and family therapists, psychologists, teachers, group leaders, etc. Depending on the role of the professional using *The Conflict Management Skills Workbook* and the specific group's needs, these sections can be used individually, combined, or implemented as part of an integrated curriculum for a more comprehensive approach.

Why use self-assessments?

Self-assessments are important in teaching various life skills. Participants will . . .

- Become aware of the primary motivators that guide behavior.
- Explore and learn to indentify potentially harmful situations.
- Explore the effects of messages received in childhood.
- Gain insight that will guide behavioral change.
- Focus thinking on behavioral goals for change.
- Uncover resources that can help to cope with problems and difficulties.
- Explore personal characteristics without judgment.
- Develop full awareness of personal strengths and weaknesses.

Because the assessments are presented in a straightforward and easy-to-use format, individuals can self-administer, score, and interpret each assessment independently.

Introduction for the Participant

This workbook will help you develop and polish the skills you need to maintain healthy relationships through effective conflict management. Conflict can be defined as a disagreement in which two or more parties perceive a threat to their interests, needs or concerns. Conflicts can be disagreements about small or very large matters, reactions to and/or a build-up of annoyances. You may encounter many types of conflict in your lifetime. Some of these conflicts revolve around relationships you have and can occur for a variety of reasons including competition over things you want or need (money, time, physical resources), the way things should operate or run (a household), or psychological issues (your perception of trust, cooperation, fairness, and respect). Regardless of the types of conflict that you are encountering, you need to be prepared to manage effectively in the conflict situations that will arise.

In every one of your relationships, you need to know how to manage conflicts that arise. Conflict management skills are probably the hardest interpersonal skills to master constructively. In conflict resolution, you must learn to work to achieve your goals, keep your cool while compromising, and work to maintain effective relationships. Conflicts often lead to a negotiating process between you and other people. You will be successful in relationships when you are able to effectively resolve conflicts in situations in which you and another person share a common interest but differ on how to achieve an outcome in which both of you get what you want.

You will be encouraged throughout this workbook to complete assessments, journaling activities and exercises. Because active involvement and doing is as important as talking about theories, it is critical that you take the time to complete all of the skill-building exercises.

The Conflict Management Skills Workbook is designed to help you learn more about yourself, identify the primary reasons you get into conflicts, and find better ways to use your newfound conflict management skills to develop and maintain happy, healthy, casual, personal, intimate and business relationships.

The Conflict Management Skills Workbook
TABLE OF CONTENTS

TABLE OF CONTENTS

SECTION I:
Beliefs about Conflict Scale

Name_____

Date_____

Beliefs about Conflict Scale Directions

Your beliefs about conflict often determine how you will react when you are confronted with a situation filled with conflict. The Beliefs About Conflict Scale will help you explore your mindset about conflict and help you determine how prepared you are to deal effectively with conflict in your life. It will be helpful to identify someone in your everyday life (partner, parent, child, co-worker) with whom you have conflict.

This scale contains 31 statements related to your personal beliefs about conflict. Read each of the statements and decide whether or not the statement describes you. If the statement is like you, circle the number next to that item under the LIKE ME column. If the statement is not like you, circle the number next to that item under the NOT LIKE ME column.

In the following example, the circled number under NOT LIKE ME indicates the statement is not true of the person completing the inventory.

	Like Me	Not Like Me
When I am in a conflict with this person . . .		
I believe that we will come to a mutually agreed upon solution	2	(1)

This is not a test and there are no right or wrong answers. Do not spend too much time thinking about your answers. Your initial response will likely be the most true for you.

Be sure to respond to every statement.

(Turn to the next page and begin)

Beliefs about Conflict Scale

I am likely to be in conflict with _____

	Like Me	Not Like Me
When I am in a conflict with this person . . .		
I believe that we will come to a mutually agreed upon solution	2	1
I find searching for a solution is frustrating to me	1	2
I rarely want to compromise	1	2
I look for win-win solutions	2	1
I see the situation as "my way versus your way"	1	2
I get angry easily	1	2
I often feel inferior to this person	1	2
I find it hard to trust this person	1	2
I like when we make a decision together	2	1
I tend to view this person as competition	1	2
I will cooperate if this person is willing to do the same	2	1
I believe that only the fittest will survive	1	2
I don't care about maintaining the relationship	1	2
I believe that in good relationships conflict can exist	2	1
I believe it is a sign of weakness to give in	1	2
I will always work to avoid conflicts	2	1

(Continued on the next page)

(Beliefs about Conflict Scale continued)

	Like Me	Not Like Me
When I am in a conflict with this person . . .		
I believe it is more important to get what I want than to be honest	1	2
I believe that compromise strengthens the relationship	2	1
I don't care about this person's perspective	1	2
I believe that everything is negotiable	2	1
I believe that brainstorming is a good way to identify solutions	2	1
I have a hard time describing what I want	1	2
I often feel intimidated by this person	1	2
I get too emotional to solve the conflict	1	2
I have a hard time understanding the nature of the conflict	1	2
I will just ignore it until it goes away	1	2
I trust the negotiation process to solve the conflict	2	1
I enjoy getting into conflicts with this person	1	2
I see our conflicts as solvable	2	1
I often can't even see the conflict in a situation	1	2
I am sure I will get blamed if there is a conflict	1	2

(Go to the Scoring Directions on the next page)

Beliefs about Conflict Scale Scoring Directions

The Beliefs about Conflict Scale is designed to measure your preconceived notions about conflict and your ability to deal effectively with it. To get your Beliefs about Conflict Scale score, total the numbers that you circled in the previous section. You will get a total from 31 to 62. Put that number in the space below.

BELIEFS ABOUT CONFLICT TOTAL = _____

Profile Interpretation

Total Scale Scores	Result	Indications
31 to 41	low	You tend to have mostly negative beliefs about conflict, about your belief in your ability to compromise and find solutions to conflict, and about your willingness to cooperate in situations that might erupt into conflict. It will be helpful to identify your negative beliefs and develop the skills to overcome them.
42 to 51	moderate	You tend to have some positive and some negative beliefs about conflict, about your belief in your ability to compromise and find solutions to conflict, and about your willingness to cooperate in situations that might erupt into conflict. It will be helpful to continue to identify your negative beliefs and work to overcome them.
52 to 62	high	You tend to have positive beliefs about conflict, about your belief in your ability to compromise and find solutions to conflict, and about your willingness to cooperate in situations that might erupt into conflict. It will be helpful to continue to identify any negative beliefs you do have.

The higher your score on this assessment, the more positive your beliefs are about dealing effectively with conflicts. If you score in the **Moderate** or **Low** range you should make efforts to ensure that you continue to work on changing your negative beliefs about conflict and begin to develop a mindset that suggests you will be willing to work cooperatively with others to settle conflicts effectively. No matter if you scored **Low**, **Moderate** or **High**, the exercises and activities that follow are designed to help you think about conflict in your life and how you view this conflict.

Identifying Situations

For effective conflict resolution, it is important to identify the situations that create conflict in your life. The following will help you to learn more about where and when most of your conflicts occur.

WHERE My Conflicts Occur

WHERE THEY OCCUR	WHY THEY OCCUR
Ex: In my house	Because my partner will not let me watch football on television.

WITH WHOM My Conflicts Occur

WITH WHOM	WHAT WE ARGUE ABOUT
Ex: My partner	*Vacation Plans*

WHEN My Conflicts Occur

WHEN THEY OCCUR	WHAT ABOUT THE SITUATION LEADS TO CONFLICT?
Ex: Going out after a sporting event	I am exhausted

Conflict Resolution Patterns

List 5 major conflicts that you can remember throughout your life.

How were these conflicts eventually resolved?

CONFLICT	WITH WHOM?	WAS IT RESOLVED?	HOW WAS THE CONFLICT RESOLVED?

What patterns do you see emerging?

_____

_____

_____

_____

_____

_____

The Conflict Resolution Process

Skills in the conflict resolution process can significantly enhance your success and happiness in your relationships. Think back to a conflict that you recently had with someone. Use the following as a format for resolving conflicts quickly and efficiently.

Describe a conflict situation you had in the past.

_____

_____

_____

_____

_____

_____

_____

_____

_____

Who is the person you were in conflict with? What is your relationship to this person?

_____

_____

_____

_____

_____

_____

_____

_____

_____

_____

_____

(Continued on the next page)

The Conflict Resolution Process *(Continued)*

Step 1 – Relating to the conflict you listed on the previous page, describe what you wanted using an "I" statement. (Focus on maintaining a positive long-term cooperative relationship with the other person.) Think about what the other person wanted in the situation.

What did you want in the situation?

_____

_____

_____

What did the other person want in the situation?

_____

_____

_____

What were your differences?

_____

_____

_____

Step 2 – Describe how you feel about the situation. Feelings need to be expressed if conflicts are to be resolved effectively.

How did you feel about the situation?

_____

_____

_____

How did the other person feel about the situation?

_____

_____

_____

(Continued on the next page)

The Conflict Resolution Process *(Continued)*

Step 3 – Explain your reasons for what you wanted in the situation. When expressing reasons, focus on wants and interests, not positions.

What were your reasons for what you wanted?

_____

_____

_____

What were the other person's reasons?

_____

_____

_____

Step 4 – Attempt to understand what the other person wanted and felt. This perspective-taking is your ability to understand how a situation appears to another person and how the person is reacting emotionally and cognitively.

What do you think the other person wanted?

_____

_____

_____

What do you think the other person thought you wanted?

_____

_____

_____

(Continued on the next page)

The Conflict Resolution Process *(Continued)*

Step 5 – Brainstorm potential agreements that would be beneficial to you and the other person. Don't judge new ideas prematurely or search for a single perfect answer.

What were some of the potential solutions that would have benefited you and the other person?

_____

_____

_____

Step 6 – Choose the agreement that seems the best for both people involved.

Which solution did you choose? How would it have met both your needs and the other person's needs?

_____

_____

_____

What did you learn from using this process?

_____

_____

_____

_____

_____

_____

_____

_____

(Continued on the next page)

 © 2010 WHOLE PERSON ASSOCIATES, 101 W. 2ND ST., SUITE 203, DULUTH MN 55802 ▪ 800-247-6789

Conflicts Can Be Beneficial

Whether you believe it or not, conflicts have the potential for positive outcomes:

1. Conflicts can clarify who you are.

How would you now describe yourself after learning more about your beliefs about conflict?

_____

_____

_____

_____

2. Conflicts can clarify what you value.

With what values do you identify?

_____

_____

_____

_____

3. Conflicts can help you pay attention to potential problems in your life.

What are some problems that you are motivated to solve?

_____

_____

_____

_____

4. Conflicts can help you clarify what you care about.

What do you care about most?

_____

_____

_____

_____

(Continued on the next page)

Conflicts Can Be Beneficial *(Continued)*

5. Conflicts can help you learn to be creative in your problem-solving.

How can conflict resolution help you be more creative?

_____

_____

_____

_____

6. Conflicts help people express their feelings.

What feelings will you be able to express using effective conflict management?

_____

_____

_____

_____

7. Conflicts can enhance your relationships.

Which relationships in your life will be enhanced using effective conflict management?

_____

_____

_____

_____

8. Conflict can highlight things that need to change in your life.

What do you feel you need to change using new conflict management skills?

_____

_____

_____

_____

Technology and Conflicts

Technology can be important in how we view conflict and conflict management. Because we communicate via technology much more than we ever have in the past, it is important to be mindful of the ways in which technology can cause conflict, or help in resolving conflicts. For the purposes of this activity, technology can include computers, the Internet, cell phones, e-mails, texting, etc.

In what ways does technology make it easier or harder to communicate?

_____

_____

_____

How do you think that technology could actually help prevent or solve conflicts?

_____

_____

_____

How do you think that technology can create more conflicts?

_____

_____

_____

How have some of your relationships improved because of technology?

_____

_____

_____

What conflicts have you had because of technology?

_____

_____

_____

What can you do to ensure that conflicts do not occur with your use of technology?

_____

_____

_____

Using Conflict Management Skills

Write about the people in your life with whom you might like to try your new conflict management skills.

_____

_____

_____

_____

_____

_____

_____

_____

_____

_____

_____

_____

What have you learned about yourself and your attitudes and beliefs about conflict?

_____

_____

_____

_____

_____

_____

_____

_____

_____

_____

_____

_____

Destructive/Constructive Conflict

How has conflict been destructive in your life?

_____

_____

_____

_____

_____

_____

_____

_____

_____

_____

_____

How can conflict be constructive in your life?

_____

_____

_____

_____

_____

_____

_____

_____

_____

_____

_____

_____

_____

Beliefs about Conflict Quotations

Choose two of the quotes below. How does each speak to your beliefs about conflict? Perhaps you will find a quote that you disagree with. Write about that also.

When we are being compassionate, we consider another's circumstance with love rather than judgment.

~ Jill Bolte Taylor

Truth springs from argument amongst friends.

~ David Hume

The stakes in conflict do not change. Battle determines who will control the wealth or its equivalent.

~ Frank Herbert

If we have no peace, it is because we have forgotten we belong to each other.

~ Mother Teresa

Change means movement. Movement means friction. Only in the frictionless vacuum of a nonexistent abstract world can movement or change occur without that abrasive friction of conflict.

~ Saul Alinsky

_____

_____

_____

_____

_____

_____

_____

_____

_____

_____

_____

_____

_____

_____

© 2010 WHOLE PERSON ASSOCIATES, 101 W. 2ND ST., SUITE 203, DULUTH MN 55802 • 800-247-6789

Indicators of a Conflicted Relationship

- Distrust

- Dishonesty

- Constant changes

- Differences in values

- Increasing lack of respect

- Desire for increased power

- Breakdowns in communication

- Small disagreements, regardless of the issues

Constructive Outcomes of Conflict

- Growth of empathy

- Clarification of problems and issues

- Development of compromise tactics

- Release emotions, feelings and stress

- Comfort in communication with others

- Establishment of cooperative behaviors

- Involvement of others in constructive problem solving

SECTION II:
Conflict Management Styles Scale

Name_____

Date_____

Conflict Management Styles Scale Directions

Conflict is an inevitable part of everyone's life. Conflict management skills are important social skills in your personal growth and development. People who are successful in life are able to manage and resolve conflict effectively.

The Conflict Management Styles Scale is designed to help you understand how you approached a recent conflict in your personal or professional life.

Write about a recent situation in which you found yourself in a conflict with another person.

_____

_____

_____

_____

_____

_____

This scale contains 50 statements divided into five conflict management styles. Read each of the statements and decide whether or not the statement best describes you. If the statement sounds like something you did in a conflict, circle the **YES**. If the statement does not sound like something you did in a conflict, circle the **NO**.

Answer the questions based on your response to the above situation.

In the following example, the circled NO indicates the statement is not true of the conflict you wrote about in the section above.

When I was in this conflict I . . .

attempted to find a middle ground   **YES**   (**NO**)

This is not a test and there are no right or wrong answers. Do not spend too much time thinking about your answers. Your initial response will likely be the most true for you. Be sure to respond to every statement. Ignore the **TOTAL** lines below each section

(Turn to the next page and begin)

Conflict Management Styles Scale

SECTION I

When I was in this conflict I ...

attempted to find a middle ground	YES	NO
gave up some of my concerns and agreed to concerns of the other person	YES	NO
kept talking until we found a solution	YES	NO
took an assertive but not domineering position	YES	NO
compromised so that we would still be friends	YES	NO
tried to negotiate	YES	NO
gave in a little to find a solution	YES	NO
offered a middle position to solve the problem	YES	NO
looked for a way to at least partially satisfy us both	YES	NO
tried to convince the other person to give up something	YES	NO

TOTAL = _____

SECTION II

When I was in this conflict I . . .

did not even consider the points of view of the other person	YES	NO
argued the merits of my position	YES	NO
firmly defended my side of the issue	YES	NO
asserted my point of view and did not cooperate	YES	NO
enjoyed debating the issue	YES	NO
stood my ground stubbornly throughout the process	YES	NO
did not worry about keeping the relationship	YES	NO
wanted to win more than anything else	YES	NO
aggressively defended my position	YES	NO
attempted to intimidate the other person	YES	NO

TOTAL = _____

(Continued on the next page)

© 2010 WHOLE PERSON ASSOCIATES, 101 W. 2ND ST., SUITE 203, DULUTH MN 55802 • 800-247-6789

(Conflict Management Styles Scale continued)

SECTION III

When I was in this conflict I . . .

avoided the person entirely	YES	NO
ignored the conflict until it went away	YES	NO
withdrew from the situation even though it hurt me to do so	YES	NO
acted in a passive way	YES	NO
let the situation resolve itself	YES	NO
postponed dealing with it for as long as possible	YES	NO
left the situation	YES	NO
accepted blame even though I knew I was right	YES	NO
admitted I was wrong, even if I didn't believe it	YES	NO
took the easiest way out of the conflict	YES	NO

TOTAL = _____

SECTION IV

When I was in this conflict I . . .

tried to meet the expectations of the other person	YES	NO
accepted what was offered by the other person	YES	NO
ignored my own goals to resolve the conflict	YES	NO
caved in	YES	NO
tried to accommodate the wishes of the other person	YES	NO
downplayed the conflict to maintain the relationship	YES	NO
gave in to the needs of the other person	YES	NO
just did what I needed to keep the peace	YES	NO
retreated to avoid hurting the feelings of the other person	YES	NO
sacrificed my own needs for those of the other person	YES	NO

TOTAL = _____

SECTION V

When I was in this conflict I . . .

worked to find solutions that are mutually acceptable	YES	NO
traded information so we could solve the problem	YES	NO
brought all concerns out into the open	YES	NO
listened to the other person's feelings	YES	NO
searched for solutions that would take both views into account	YES	NO
tried for a "win-win" solution	YES	NO
wasn't worried about how long it took to find the best solution	YES	NO
enjoyed the open discussions of the issues	YES	NO
wanted both sides to be satisfied	YES	NO
learned a lot and shared information with the other person	YES	NO

TOTAL = _____

(Go to the Scoring Directions on the next page)

Conflict Management Styles Scale
Scoring Directions

For conflicts to be resolved, they must be managed. Everyone has a unique, personal style when it comes to managing conflicts. The Conflict Management Style Scale is designed to help you explore your style in handling a recent conflict. Count the number of YES's you circled and write the total below each section.

Then, transfer your totals in each of the five sections to the lines below:

SECTION I   TOTAL   =   _____ (Compromising)

SECTION II   TOTAL   =   _____ (Competing)

SECTION III TOTAL   =   _____ (Avoiding)

SECTION IV   TOTAL   =   _____ (Giving-In)

SECTION V   TOTAL   =   _____ (Collaborating)

People differ in their ways of communicating, their political and religious views, and their different cultural backgrounds. In a diverse society, these differences often lead to conflicts. When you are in conflict with another person, you will discover no one style fits or works in every situation. Each of the five styles can be useful in different situations. Many of us rely on, and feel comfortable, using one style more often than the others. The area in which you scored the highest tends to be the conflict management style you probably use most often. Similarly, the area in which you scored the lowest tends to be your least used conflict management style. Go to the next page to learn more about the various conflict management styles.

Profile Interpretation

Total Scale Scores	Result	Indications
7 to 10	high	Scores from 7 to 10 on any single scale indicate that you have many of the characteristics of people with that conflict management style.
4 to 6	moderate	Scores from 4 to 6 on any single scale indicate that you have some of the characteristics of people with that conflict management style.
0 to 3	low	Scores from 0 to 3 on any single scale indicate that you do not have many of the characteristics of people with that conflict management style.

Compromising – *Profile Interpretation*

People with a Compromising Conflict Management Style try to find a solution that will partially satisfy everyone. This is often called the middle-ground approach because participants are willing to negotiate and come up with a compromise in the situation in which both people feel satisfied. They may also be willing to sacrifice the compatibility of their relationship with others in order to reach an agreement. They give a little to get a little, and they believe that both sides should make concessions in order to reach a resolution. They have discovered that it is important to back off from some issues in order to gain on other issues.

What I like about this style:

_____

_____

_____

_____

_____

What I don't like about this style:

_____

_____

_____

_____

_____

When does this style work, or not work?

_____

_____

_____

_____

_____

The Compromising Style Can Serve in a Variety of Situations

The Compromising Style can be used when there are important or complex issues that have no clear or simple solutions. For you, what would these situations include?

_____

_____

_____

_____

The Compromising Style can be used when all people have strong interests in different solutions. For you, what would these situations include?

_____

_____

_____

_____

The Compromising Style can be used when there are no time constraints. For you, what would these situations include?

_____

_____

_____

_____

In which situations in your life would you use the Compromising Style?

_____

_____

_____

_____

Competing – *Profile Interpretation*

People with a Competing Conflict Management Style attempt to achieve their goals at all costs and as quickly as they possibly can. They take a firm stand and know what they want. They usually insist that the other people let them have their way, regardless of how much it affects their relationships with others. They operate from a position of power and are usually more concerned with having their way than with the feelings of others. No matter what the cost, winning is the most important thing for them. The use of this style can leave people feeling unsatisfied and resentful.

What I like about this style:

_____

_____

_____

_____

_____

What I don't like about this style:

_____

_____

_____

_____

_____

When does this style work, or not work?

_____

_____

_____

_____

_____

_____

_____

The Competing Style Can Serve in a Variety of Situations

The Competing Style can be used when maintaining supportive relationships is not critical. For you, what would these situations include?

_____

_____

_____

_____

The Competing Style can be used when others may take advantage of non-competitive behavior by you. For you, what would these situations include?

_____

_____

_____

_____

The Competing Style can be used when a conflict must be settled quickly. For you, what would these situations include?

_____

_____

_____

_____

In which situations in your life would you use this style?

_____

_____

_____

_____

_____

Avoiding – *Profile Interpretation*

People with an Avoiding Conflict Management Style usually are willing to give up their own goals to maintain relationships with other people. They would rather hide from and ignore conflict than resolve it. They may give up personal goals and display passive behavior creating a personal loss situation. To do so, they generally avoid conflicts within important relationships. They may avoid other conflicts by physically removing themselves from the environment or by not coming into contact with the others who represent the potential for conflict. They may avoid others psychologically by not speaking or by ignoring them and another conflict situation, and subsequently, the conflict often goes unresolved.

What I like about this style:

_____

_____

_____

_____

_____

What I don't like about this style:

_____

_____

_____

_____

_____

When does this style work, or not work?

_____

_____

_____

_____

_____

The Avoiding Style Can Serve in a Variety of Situations

The Avoiding Style can be used when confrontation will hurt a good relationship. For you, what would these situations include?

_____

_____

_____

_____

The Avoiding Style can be used when others could more effectively resolve the conflict. For you, what would these situations include?

_____

_____

_____

_____

The Avoiding Style can be used when a disruption outweighs the consequences of resolving the conflict. For you, what would these situations include?

_____

_____

_____

_____

In which situations in your life would you use this style?

_____

_____

_____

_____

_____

Giving-In – *Profile Interpretation*

People with a Giving-In Conflict Management Style usually give up their personal and professional goals so that other people can achieve their goals. They usually value their relationships with others so much that they attempt to smooth over the situation and give them their way. For them, the goal is often of no importance but the relationship with the others is of high importance. By giving in, they avoid the risk of a confrontation so they can continue to get along with the other people.

What I like about this style:

_____

_____

_____

_____

_____

What I don't like about this style:

_____

_____

_____

_____

_____

When does this style work, or not work?

_____

_____

_____

_____

_____

_____

_____

The Giving-In Style Can Serve in a Variety of Situations

The Giving-In Style can be used when you want to maintain the relationship at all costs. For you, what would these situations include?

_____

_____

_____

_____

The Giving-In Style can be used when suggestions are not important to the other person. For you, what would these situations include?

_____

_____

_____

_____

The Giving-In Style can be used to minimize losses in situations where you are outmatched or losing ground. For you, what would these situations include?

_____

_____

_____

_____

In which situations in your life would you use this style?

_____

_____

_____

_____

_____

Collaborating – *Profile Interpretation*

People with a Collaborating Conflict Management Style tend to want to meet the needs of all people involved in the conflict. They can be highly assertive, but are more than willing to cooperate effectively and acknowledge the importance of everyone involved. They are interested in bringing together a variety of viewpoints to get the best possible solution for everyone. They want all sides to be satisfied. They support open discussions, brainstorming and creative problem solving to come to a consensus.

What I like about this style:

_____

_____

_____

_____

_____

What I don't like about this style:

_____

_____

_____

_____

_____

When does this style work, or not work?

_____

_____

_____

_____

_____

_____

_____

The Collaborating Style Can Serve in a Variety of Situations

The Collaborating Style can be used when you are in conflict with one or more of your peers, team members or colleagues. For you, what would these situations include?

_____

_____

_____

_____

The Collaborating Style can be used when you are trying to merge several different perspectives. For you, what would these situations include?

_____

_____

_____

_____

The Collaborating Style can be used when you are trying to gain commitment and support of everyone involved. For you, what would these situations include?

_____

_____

_____

_____

In which situations in your life would you use this style?

_____

_____

_____

_____

_____

My Conflict History

How conflict was managed in your home may be affecting how you manage conflict in your life. Answer the following questions related to conflict in your family-of-origin.

With whom was your mother (or female caregiver) in conflict? Describe her conflict situations.

_____

_____

_____

How would you describe how your mother (or female caregiver) handled conflict?

_____

_____

_____

With whom was your father (or male caregiver) in conflict? Describe his conflict situations.

_____

_____

_____

How would you describe how your father (or male caregiver) handled conflict?

_____

_____

_____

How would you describe how you handled conflict with your parents?

_____

_____

_____

If you have siblings, how do they manage conflict in their lives?

_____

_____

_____

(Continued on the next page)

My Conflict History *(Continued)*

How would you describe how you handled conflict with your siblings?

_____

_____

_____

When you were young, what verbal or nonverbal messages did you receive about how to manage conflict?

_____

_____

_____

How does the conflict management style of your parents affect you now?

_____

_____

How is your conflict management style similar to, or different from, that of your father (or male caregiver)?

_____

_____

How is your conflict management style similar to, or different from, that of your mother (or female caregiver)?

_____

_____

As a child or teen, with whom did you (or do you) have conflicts?

_____

_____

As a child or teen, how did you (or do you) handle these conflicts?

_____

_____

_____

How Effective is My Conflict Management Style?

Describe how your conflict management style has helped you in resolving conflicts.

_____

_____

_____

_____

_____

_____

_____

_____

_____

_____

_____

Describe how your conflict management style has hurt you in resolving conflicts.

_____

_____

_____

_____

_____

_____

_____

_____

_____

_____

_____

_____

Using the Five Conflict Management Styles

How will you use the five various conflict management styles below to help you the next time you encounter a conflict in your personal, school or professional life?

- Compromising
- Competing
- Avoiding
- Giving-In
- Collaborating

_____

_____

_____

_____

_____

_____

_____

_____

_____

_____

_____

_____

_____

_____

_____

_____

_____

_____

_____

_____

_____

_____

_____

Conflict Management Quotations

Place check marks by the quotes that you feel would inspire you to manage conflicts effectively and also work to help other people settle their conflicts. You can cut the quote out and post by your computer or on your refrigerator or tuck it into your wallet. At the bottom of the page, write why those particular quotes speak to you.

Peace is not the absence of conflict but the presence of creative alternatives for responding to conflict — alternatives to passive or aggressive responses, alternatives to violence.

~ Dorothy Thompson

The direct use of force is such a poor solution to any problem; it is generally employed only by small children and large nations.

~ David Friedman

We are not going to deal with the violence in our communities, our homes, and our nation, until we learn to deal with the basic ethic of how we resolve our disputes and to place an emphasis on peace in the way we relate to one another.

~ Marian Wright Edelman

Non-cooperation is a measure of discipline and sacrifice, and it demands respect f or the opposite views.

~ Mohandas K. Gandhi

Difficulties are meant to rouse, not discourage. The human spirit is to grow strong by conflict.
~ William Ellery Channing

You can't shake hands with a clenched fist.

~ Indira Gandhi

True peace is not merely the absence of tension: it is the presence of justice.
~ Martin Luther King Jr.

I selected the quotation(s) above because

_____

_____

_____

_____

_____

_____

_____

_____

_____

_____

Conflict Management Process Steps

Step 1 – Describe what you want.

Step 2 – Describe how you feel about the situation.

Step 3 – Explain your reason for what you want in the situation.

Step 4 – Attempt to understand what the other person wants and feels.

Step 5 – Brainstorm potential agreements that would be beneficial to you and the other person.

Step 6 – Choose the agreement that seems the best for both.

Step 7 – Agree to abide by the conditions of the agreement.

Causes of Conflict

- Power

- Differences in beliefs

- Desire for participation

- Repetitive negative behaviors

- Money and physical resources

- Inequality of treatment by others

- Poor communication in relationships

- Misperceptions of fairness and respect

SECTION III:
Listening for Meaning Scale

Name_____

Date_____

Listening for Meaning Scale Directions

Whether you are trying to resolve a conflict between two parties, or attempting to avoid or resolve a conflict yourself, you need effective active listening skills. Active listening is listening to more than the words that are being said – it is listening and observing the meaning behind the words. The Listening For Meaning Scale was designed to help you examine how effective you are in listening for meaning and understanding during times of conflict.

This assessment contains 24 statements related to active listening. Read each of the statements and decide whether or not the statement describes you. If the statement is true, circle the number next to that item under the TRUE column. If the statement is false, circle the number next to that item under the FALSE column.

In the following example, the circled number under FALSE indicates the statement is not true of the person completing the inventory.

When I am talking with another person . . .

	TRUE	FALSE
I make appropriate eye contact	2	(1)

This is not a test and there are no right or wrong answers. Do not spend too much time thinking about your answers. Your initial response will likely be the most true for you. Be sure to respond to every statement.

(Turn to the next page and begin)

Listening for Meaning Scale

When I am talking with another person . . .	TRUE	FALSE
BODY LANGUAGE		
I make appropriate eye contact	2	1
I hardly notice body language and tone of voice	1	2
I maintain open body posture	2	1
I lean a little toward the person who is speaking	2	1
I rarely nod my head to show understanding	1	2
I reassure and support the other person	2	1
	TOTAL = _____	
ATTENDING		
I listen with my full attention	2	1
I finish the other person's sentences	1	2
I try to understand what the other person is saying	2	1
I am constantly comparing myself to the other person	1	2
I try to read the other person's mind	1	2
I try not to interrupt	2	1
	TOTAL = _____	
RESPONDING		
I think about other things while the person is talking	1	2
I mentally plan my response while the other person is talking	1	2
I do not judge the person ahead of time	2	1
I am easily distracted	1	2
I focus on specific points and shut out the rest of the message	1	2
I find myself daydreaming	1	2
	TOTAL = _____	
LISTENING FOR UNDERSTANDING		
I listen for feelings as well as content	2	1
I ask for clarification if I do not understand something	2	1
I hear what I want to hear	1	2
I attempt to understand the underlying meaning of the words	2	1
I always seem to understand the other person's position	2	1
I let the other person know I heard what was said	2	1
	TOTAL = _____	

(Go to the Scoring Directions on the next page)

Listening for Meaning Scale
Scoring Directions

The Listening for Meaning Scale is designed to measure how proficient you are at listening to others, to avoid your own conflicts or to help others who are engaged in a conflict. At the bottom of each of the categories on the previous page, add the numbers that you circled. Then transfer your totals below.

Body Language Total   =   _____

Attending Total   =   _____

Responding Total   =   _____

Listening for Understanding Total   =   _____

Profile Interpretation

Scores on the Listening for Meaning Scale range from 6 to 12.

Total Scale Scores	Result	Indications
11 to 12	high	**If you scored between 11 and 12 on any scale**, you are an active listener and go out of your way to truly hear what the other person is saying, ask questions for more information, and paraphrase important points back to the communicator.
8 to 10	moderate	**If you scored between 8 and 10**, you are an average listener, and you will benefit by further developing your active listening and responding skills.
6 to 7	low	**If your score was between 6 and 7**, the following exercises will assist you in developing your active listening and responding skills.

Regardless of your score on the assessment, all of the following exercises have been designed to help you increase your listening skills.

Building Your Listening Skills

Active listening is a life skill to learn and master. An active listener can settle personal conflicts with other people and help others settle their conflicts.

The following exercises are designed to help you to begin thinking about your potential blocks to active listening and to take steps to listen more effectively.

ACTIVE LISTENING SKILLS

Active listening is a way of listening and responding that dramatically improves mutual understanding and enhances relationships with others. People often talk to one another, but they do not listen attentively, or at all. People talking to one another often get distracted or think about what they are going to say next. They may not listen for the meaning behind the words being spoken. This is especially true when people are in conflict with one another. Many times people in conflict are so worried about trying to win an argument, or get their point across, that they do not hear accurately what the other person is saying. Active listening is of critical importance in managing and resolving conflicts.

Active listening is a form of listening and responding that focuses attention on the speaker. In active listening, you as the listener are required to fully attend to what the other person is saying, repeat in your own words what you think the other person is saying, and determine if you have understood correctly. It sounds easy, doesn't it? Well it is if you know the active listening process and you practice using active listening in your daily activities.

ACTIVE LISTENING WITH ANOTHER PERSON

Specific successful active listening skills can be learned and practiced. Some of these skills are related to listening and some are related to responding effectively once you have heard what was said. Active listening involves much more than hearing and speaking to another person - it is communicating for true understanding. Some active listening skills are included in the next section. Practice them with another person.

Active Listening Skills Practice

1) Communicate to another that you are listening

To listen actively, be aware of your body language.

- Maintain eye contact with the person
- Keep your arms unfolded and uncrossed to maintain an open body posture
- Lean forward a little toward the person if you are sitting
- Move closer to the person, without going into personal space
- Nod to show understanding
- Say things like "yes" or "uh huh"
- Keep distractions to a minimum

Practice these skills with a partner. How did it feel?

_____

_____

_____

2) Ask questions

To listen actively, you need to ask good questions. Practice this skill with a partner.

Open questions solicit as much information about a topic as possible.
   ("What did you do this weekend?" "How is your father doing?")

Closed questions ask for one-word or short answers.
   ("How old are you?" "Did you like the movie?")

Avoid "Why" questions as much as possible; they force the listener to make interpretations which may not be productive in the resolution of conflict. (Instead, try *"In what way . . ."*)

What did you learn from this exercise?

_____

_____

_____

_____

_____

(Continued on the next page)

Active Listening Skills Practice *(Continued)*

3) Responding effectively

To listen actively, you need to be able to respond effectively to the other person. Some techniques that can help you to resolve conflicts:

Paraphrasing

Reflection of feelings

Clarifying

PARAPHRASING

Paraphrasing lets other people know you are trying to understand their point of view. It clarifies communication, reduces emotional intensity, elicits additional information and assures understanding of the conflict. When you paraphrase, restate in your own words what you think the other person just said.

To begin your paraphrases, you need a lead-in statement that alerts the other person that you are not trying to tell them how to feel. You are simply restating in your own words what the other person said. In actuality, you are assuring the other person that you are trying to understand and affirm what you heard. Lead-in statements:

"What I am hearing you say is . . ."

"It sounds like . . ."

"Am I correct to say that . . ."

"So, in other words . . ."

Practice this skill with a partner. Take turns telling each other about your day. While you are talking, your partner will paraphrase your statements. Similarly, while your partner is talking, you will paraphrase your partner's statements.

How did you feel when your partner was paraphrasing your statements? What did you learn?

_____

_____

_____

How did you feel when you were paraphrasing your partner's statements? What did you learn?

_____

_____

_____

(Responding Effectively continued on the next page)

Responding Effectively *(Continued)*

PARAPHRASING

In the right-hand column in the table below, write a paraphrase for the statement in the left-hand column.

WHAT SOMEONE IN CONFLICT MIGHT SAY	YOUR PARAPHRASE
"I don't like it when you stay out so late"	
"I want you to take care of the kids more"	
"You need to help me write this report"	
"If you ever do that again, I will walk out!"	
"I want the table over there"	

(Responding Effectively continued on the next page)

Responding Effectively *(Continued)*

REFLECTION OF FEELINGS

Listening to and reflecting feelings back to the other person is critical in active listening. To be an effective reflector of feelings, restate what the person has said to you much like paraphrasing, but you focus on the feelings. So if someone would say to you "I am excited about the vacation we are taking," you could reflect feelings by restating something like "You sound relieved about not having to work for two weeks!" In the right-hand column in the table that follows, write a reflection of feelings for the statement in the left-hand column.

WHAT SOMEONE IN CONFLICT MIGHT SAY	YOUR REFLECTION
"I hate when you leave your clothes lying around"	
"I'm turning 32 tomorrow"	
"The boss said that my sales numbers are down this month"	
"I don't like to drive in the dark"	
"I don't know if I can study anymore"	

(Responding Effectively continued on the next page)

Responding Effectively *(Continued)*

CLARIFYING

When clarifying, you tell the other person what you thought you heard, learn whether you were right or wrong, and then ask questions for more clarification. You are checking your assumptions and verifying the meaning intended by the other person.

Examples of clarifiers:

> *"I'm not sure what you meant when you said . . ."*
>
> *"Please tell me more about . . ."*
>
> *"Please explain what you meant by . . ."*
>
> *"Can you give me an example of that . . ."*
>
> *"Please tell me a little bit more about . . ."*

Notice that clarifiers help the listener to better understand what the speaker is trying to say.

> Speaker: *"He makes me so angry when he shows up late."*
>
> Listener: *"You think that he takes you for granted. Is that right?"*
>
> Speaker: *"Yes and no!"*
>
> Listener: *"Can you tell me a little bit more?"*

Practice this skill with a partner. Pick a topic of concern to both of you but that is not more than a mild source of conflict. Discuss the topic, taking turns being the speaker and the listener. When you are the listener, ask questions to clarify what you do not understand. Continue clarifying until your partner feels completely heard and understood. Then switch places and do the exercise again with a new topic.

How did you feel when your partner was clarifying your statements? What did you learn?

_____

_____

_____

How did you feel when you were clarifying your partner's statements? What did you learn?

_____

_____

_____

(Responding Effectively continued on the next page)

Responding Effectively *(Continued)*
CLARIFYING PRACTICE

In the right-hand column in the table that follows, write a clarification for the statement in the left-hand column.

WHAT SOMEONE IN CONFLICT MIGHT SAY	YOUR CLARIFICATION
"You just try to make me angry"	
"She always leaves the bedroom in a mess"	
"You've ruined my weekend"	
"Dogs are more trouble than they are worth"	
"You spend way too much money on yourself"	

Blocks to Active Listening

Active listening roadblocks that could interfere with your communication and conflict resolution:

- Giving Advice
- Patronizing
- Quick Reassurance
- Filtering
- Preaching
- Interrupting
- Sparring
- Rehearsing

Giving Advice *("I think that you would be better off to . . ." or "I advise you to . . .")*

When you find yourself giving advice, with whom are you talking?

_____

What is the conversation usually about?

_____

_____

_____

Why do you give advice to this person?

_____

_____

_____

Preaching *("You should . . ." or "You shouldn't . . .")*

When you find yourself preaching, with whom are you talking?

_____

What is the conversation usually about?

_____

_____

_____

Why do you preach to this person?

_____

_____

_____

(Continued on the next page)

Blocks to Active Listening *(Continued)*

Patronizing *("You poor thing . . . or "Oh, don't worry about it, it's very complicated.")*

When you find yourself patronizing, with whom are you talking?

_____

What is the conversation usually about?

_____

_____

_____

Why do you patronize this person?

_____

_____

_____

Interrupting (Cutting people off before they can finish what they are saying.)

When you find yourself interrupting, with whom are you talking?

_____

What is the conversation usually about?

_____

_____

_____

Why do you interrupt this person?

_____

_____

_____

(Continued on the next page)

Blocks to Active Listening (Continued)

Quick Reassurance ("Don't worry" or "It will be better soon")

When you find yourself being too quick to reassure, with whom are you talking?

_____

What is the conversation usually about?

_____

_____

_____

Why are you so quick to reassure this person?

_____

_____

_____

Sparring (Using sarcasm or insults _"Now, isn't that a really useful idea!"_ or, after a long night of tossing and turning, _"Well, don't you look just bright and shiny this morning."_)

When you find yourself being sarcastic or insulting, with whom are you talking?

_____

What is the conversation usually about?

_____

_____

_____

Why are you sparring with this person?

_____

_____

_____

(Continued on the next page)

Blocks to Active Listening *(Continued)*

Filtering – (Tuning out certain topics that you are not interested in.)

When you find yourself filtering conversations, with whom are you talking?

_____

What is the conversation usually about?

_____
_____
_____

Why do you filter conversations with this person?

_____
_____
_____

Rehearsing – (Mentally planning your response to what someone is saying while the other person is still speaking.)

When you find yourself rehearsing, with whom are you talking?

_____

What is the conversation usually about?

_____
_____
_____

Why are you rehearsing with this person?

_____
_____
_____

Listening

Why is listening so important in conflict situations?

_____

_____

_____

_____

_____

_____

_____

_____

_____

_____

How will you guard against the blocks to active listening?

_____

_____

_____

_____

_____

_____

_____

_____

_____

_____

_____

My Strengths and Weaknesses

What are your strengths when listening to other people?

_____

_____

_____

_____

_____

_____

_____

_____

_____

_____

_____

_____

What are your weaknesses when listening to other people?

_____

_____

_____

_____

_____

_____

_____

_____

_____

_____

_____

_____

_____

Listening for Meaning Quotations

Choose two quotations below. On the lines that follow each of them, describe what the quotes mean to you and how it relates to your ability to listen for meaning.

I know that you believe you understand what you think I said, but I'm not sure you realize that what you hear is not what I meant.

~ Robert McCloskey

_____

_____

_____

Deep listening is miraculous for both the listener and speaker.
When someone receives us with open-hearted, non-judging, intensely interested listening, our spirits expand.

~ Sue Patton Thoele

_____

_____

_____

The first duty of love is to listen.

~ Paul Tillich

_____

_____

_____

Listening is a magnetic and strange thing, a creative force. When we really listen to people there is an alternating current, and this recharges us so that we never get tired of each other. We are constantly being re-created.

~ Brenda Ueland

_____

_____

_____

I like to listen. I have learned a great deal from listening carefully.
Most people never listen.

~ Ernest Hemingway

_____

_____

_____

Five Steps to Active Listening

- Face the other person

- Open your posture

- Lean slightly towards the person

- Maintain eye contact

- Relax while listening to the person

An Active Listener

FOCUS ON THESE CLUES:

- What the person is saying

- How it is being said

- The person's view of the topic

- The emotions expressed

- What the person is trying to achieve

- The person's body language

80

SECTION IV:
Hot Buttons Scale

Name_____

Date_____

Hot Buttons Scale Directions

Conflict triggers are your personal *hot buttons* that it seems people push to engage you in conflict. In reality, *hot buttons* come from within you, not really from someone or some external situation pressing them. When you perceive a threat to some part of your identity, you are triggered to respond.

This assessment contains 30 statements related to what triggers conflict for you. Read each of the statements and decide whether or not the statement describes you. If the statement *does* describe you, circle the number in the **YES** column. If the statement *does not* describe you, circle the number in the **NO** column.

In the following example, the circled number under **YES** indicates the statement is descriptive of the person completing the inventory.

	YES	NO	
I get into conflicts mostly when someone . . .			
Does not give me the respect I deserve	(2)	1	(R)

This is not a test and there are no right or wrong answers. Do not spend too much time thinking about your answers. Your initial response will likely be the most true for you. Be sure to respond to every statement.

(Turn to the next page and begin)

Hot Buttons Scale

	YES	NO	
I get into conflicts mostly when someone . . .			
Does not give me the respect I deserve	2	1	(R)
Does not acknowledge my accomplishments	2	1	(R)
Does not value my contribution	2	1	(R)
Does not recognize what I have to offer	2	1	(R)
Does not treat me fairly	2	1	(R)
Does not include me	2	1	(R)

R Total = _____

Criticizes me	2	1	(C)
Makes fun of me	2	1	(C)
Censures what I say	2	1	(C)
Passes judgment on me	2	1	(C)
Speaks poorly of me behind my back	2	1	(C)
Gives me negative feedback	2	1	(C)

C Total = _____

Tells me what to do	2	1	(I)
Holds power over me	2	1	(I)
Tries to rule what I do	2	1	(I)
Holds me back	2	1	(I)
Takes control away from me	2	1	(I)
Manipulates me	2	1	(I)

I Total = _____

Tries to cheat me	2	1	(P)
Takes my things without my consent	2	1	(P)
Withholds from me what I need	2	1	(P)
Gain what I want	2	1	(P)
Leaves me without the resources I need	2	1	(P)
Receives more than I do	2	1	(P)

P Total = _____

Makes unrealistic demands of me	2	1	(H)
Maintains flexibility	2	1	(H)
Threatens me or others	2	1	(H)
Uses hostile humor	2	1	(H)
Ignores me	2	1	(H)
Manipulates me with nasty or rude comments	2	1	(H)

H Total = _____

(Go to the Scoring Directions on the next page)

Hot Buttons Scale Scoring Directions

The Hot Buttons Scale is designed to help you identify the situations that trigger conflict reactions for you. For the first group of items on the previous two pages, add the numbers that you circled that are indicated with an (R). This will allow you to get your Respect score. You will get a total in the range from 6 to 12. Put that number in the space marked next to the word **Respect** below. Do the same for the others. Then transfer these totals to the spaces below:

(R) Respect Total = _____

(C) Criticizes Total = _____

(I) Influence Total = _____

(P) Physical Resources Total = _____

(H) Hostility Total = _____

Profile Interpretation

Total Scale Scores	Result	Indications
11 to 12	high	**If you scored between 11 and 12 on any scale**, this area tends to have hot button issues for you and probably leads to conflicts with other people.
8 to 10	moderate	**If you scored between 8 and 10**, this area tends to have some hot button issues that can sometimes lead to conflicts with other people.
6 to 7	low	**If your score was between 6 and 7**, this area tends to have very few hot button issues that can lead to conflicts with other people.

Regardless of your scores on the assessment, the following exercises have been designed to help you explore your *hot buttons* and gain more insight into the types of things that erupt into conflict in your everyday life.

Respect

Respect is a feeling of esteem for another person, followed by actions and conduct that represent this feeling of esteem. In the following table, in the left-hand column, list the people whom you respect and in the right-hand column, explain how you show them that respect.

People I Respect

PEOPLE I RESPECT	HOW I SHOW RESPECT TO THEM
My next door neighbor	*When I am around him, I always listen to the stories he tells me about his prisoner-of-war experiences. His stories symbolize his patriotism.*

People I Do Not Respect

In the following table, in the left-hand column, list the people whom you do not respect and in the right-hand column, explain why you have this lack of respect.

PEOPLE I DO NOT RESPECT	WHY I LACK RESPECT
My supervisor at work	She does not give me credit for projects; rather she takes credit for things I do.

Respect Summary

Take a look at the first table you just completed, *People I Respect*, and answer the following questions:

What themes do you see when you look at the table of people you respect (are they people at work, home, school, etc.?)

_____

_____

_____

_____

What are the qualities or actions of the people you respect?

_____

_____

_____

_____

Look at the second table you just completed, *People I Do Not Respect*, and answer the following questions:

What themes do you see when you look at the table of people whom you do not respect (are they people at work, home, school, etc.?)

_____

_____

_____

_____

What are the qualities or actions of the people that you cannot respect?

_____

_____

_____

_____

Criticism

When people are critical of others, it often leads to conflict. In the following table, list in the left-hand column the people who criticize you and in the right-hand column, how they are critical of you.

PEOPLE WHO CRITICIZE ME	HOW THEY CRITICIZE ME

Criticism Summary

Think of a particular person who is critical of you.

_____

How do you feel when that person criticizes you?

_____

_____

_____

In what ways does it bother you? Why?

_____

_____

_____

What do you do when it happens?

_____

_____

_____

Why do you care about that person being critical of you?

_____

_____

_____

What types of conflicts erupt from these acts of criticism?

_____

_____

_____

_____

Influence and Control

When people try to influence and control how others act and behave, it often leads to conflict. In the following table, in the left-hand column list the people who try to influence and control you. In the right-hand column, explain what they do.

PEOPLE WHO TRY TO INFLUENCE AND CONTROL ME	WHAT DOES THE PERSON DO?

Influence and Control Summary

How do you feel when people try to influence and control you?

_____

_____

_____

_____

Why does it bother you so much?

_____

_____

_____

What do you do when it happens?

_____

_____

_____

_____

Why do you think people do that to you?

_____

_____

_____

_____

What types of conflicts erupt from these controlling behaviors?

_____

_____

_____

_____

Physical Resources

When people do not have enough physical resources, or other people try to take a person's resources, it often leads to conflict. In the following table, in the left-hand column list the people who take or use your resources without your consent and in the right-hand column describe how they do that and what they take.

PEOPLE WHO TAKE MY RESOURCES WITHOUT MY CONSENT	HOW DO THEY DO IT? WHAT DO THEY TAKE?

Physical Resources Summary

How do you feel when people try to take your physical resources?

_____

_____

_____

_____

Think of a particular person who does that excessively? Why does the person do that?

_____

_____

_____

_____

Why do you think that person does that to you?

_____

_____

_____

_____

What do you do when it happens?

_____

_____

_____

_____

What types of conflicts erupt from these situations?

_____

_____

_____

_____

Hostility

When people are hostile to others, it often leads to conflict. In the following table, in the left-hand column, list the people who are hostile to you and in the right-hand column, list what they do to show their hostility.

PEOPLE WHO ARE HOSTILE TOWARD ME	HOW THEY SHOW THEIR HOSTILITY

Hostility Summary

How do you feel when people are hostile toward you?

_____

_____

_____

Think of someone whose hostility particularly bothers you? Why does it bother you so much?

_____

_____

_____

Why do you think the person behaves this way toward you?

_____

_____

_____

_____

What do you do when it happens?

_____

_____

_____

_____

What types of conflicts erupt from these acts of hostility?

_____

_____

_____

_____

My Triggers

What you have learned about yourself and the types of actions or behaviors that trigger conflicts for you.

_____

_____

_____

_____

_____

_____

_____

_____

_____

_____

_____

What you have learned about yourself and the types of actions or behaviors that DO NOT trigger conflicts for you.

_____

_____

_____

_____

_____

_____

_____

_____

_____

_____

_____

_____

Handling Hot Button Issues

How will you now work to handle hot button issues so that they do not flare up into conflicts?

_____

_____

_____

_____

_____

_____

_____

_____

_____

_____

_____

_____

_____

_____

_____

_____

_____

_____

_____

_____

_____

_____

_____

_____

_____

_____

_____

Hot Buttons Quotations

Choose two of the quotes below. How does each speak to you about your triggers (hot buttons) for conflict? Perhaps you will find a quote that you disagree with. Write about it also.

There is no squabbling so violent as that between people who accepted an idea yesterday and those who will accept the same idea tomorrow.

~ Christopher Morley

If you can't make the image bigger or more important than what you see, then don't push the button.

~ Ruth Bernhard

Whenever two good people argue over principles, they are both right.

~ Marie Ebner Von Eschenbach

Everybody has a hot button. Who is pushing yours? While you probably cannot control that person, you CAN control the way you react.

~ Anonymous

Conflict is the beginning of consciousness.

~ M. Esther Harding

Don't be afraid of opposition. Remember, a kite rises against, not with the wind.
~ Hamilton Mabie

_____

_____

_____

_____

_____

_____

_____

_____

_____

_____

_____

_____

Deal With Hot Button Issues:

- Tell others how it makes you feel.

- Make personal statements using I and mine.

- Establish the legitimacy of your wants and needs.

- Believe that you have a perfect right for respect.

- Focus on getting what you want, while preserving the relationship.

- Communicate clearly and descriptively.

- Negotiate when possible.

Deal with Negative Feelings

- Express your angry feelings.

- Do not conceal your feelings.

- Express your anger constructively.

- Accept negative feelings as natural and normal.

- Do not be impulsive when expressing anger.

- Be aware of your body language.

SECTION V:
Negotiation Style Scale

Name_____

Date_____

Negotiation Style Scale Directions

In some situations, it is necessary to negotiate for what you want and need. People negotiate for all kinds of reasons such as where to go on vacation, how to divide household chores and how to divide tasks on projects at work or school.

To be an effective negotiator, you need to become aware of how you negotiate, and learn to recognize the way the people you are dealing with does their negotiating. The Negotiation Style Scale is designed to help you understand your present approach to negotiating with other people and to help you improve, if needed. This booklet contains 40 words that are divided into four negotiation styles. Read each word and decide if the word describes you. If it does describe you, circle that word. If it does not describe you, do not circle the word.

Are you more . . .

(Analytical (A))	Diplomatic (C)	Headstrong (B)	Patient (C)
Animated (D)	Dominating (B)	(Impulsive (D))	Practical (A)
Assertive (B)	Dynamic (B)	Independent (B)	Productive (B)

In the above examples, the circled words "Analytical" and "Impulsive" describe the person completing the assessment. You will later be asked to count the words you've circled for each of the four sections and add the total words circled in each column to determine your scores.

This is not a test and there are no right or wrong answers. Do not spend too much time thinking about your answers. Your initial response will likely be the most true for you. Be sure to respond to every statement

(Turn to the next page and begin)

Negotiation Style Scale

Check all the terms that describe you . . .

Analytical (A)	Diplomatic (C)	Headstrong (B)	Patient (C)
Animated (D)	Dominating (B)	Impulsive (D)	Practical (A)
Assertive (B)	Dynamic (B)	Independent (B)	Productive (B)
Calm (C)	Energetic (D)	Inspiring (D)	Quiet (A)
Careful (A)	Enthusiastic (D)	Logical (A)	Relationship Oriented (C)
Confident (B)	Even Tempered (A)	Low-Key (A)	Reserved (C)
Decisive (B)	Fast-Paced (D)	Open (C)	Results Oriented (B)
Dependable (C)	Flamboyant (D)	Opinionated (D)	Supportive (C)
Detached (C)	Forceful (B)	Optimistic (D)	Task Oriented (A)
Detail Oriented (A)	Gentle (C)	Orderly (A)	Visionary (D)

TOTALS:

A. _____

B. _____

C. _____

D. _____

(Go to the Scoring Directions on the next page)

Negotiation Style Scale Scoring Directions

On the scale, count the words you circled for each letter, A, B, C and D. Put that total on the appropriate line below the words. Then transfer your totals to these lines below:

SECTION A "TOTAL" = _____ (Analytical)

SECTION B "TOTAL" = _____ (Driven)

SECTION C "TOTAL" = _____ (Amiable)

SECTION D "TOTAL" = _____ (Expressive)

Profile Interpretation

Total Scale Scores	Result	Indications
7 to 10	high	**Scores from 7 to 10** on any single scale indicate that you have many of the characteristics of people with that negotiation style.
4 to 6	moderate	**Scores from 4 to 6** on any single scale indicate that you do have some of the characteristics of people with that negotiation style.
0 to 3	low	**Scores from 0 to 3** on any single scale indicate that you do not have many of the characteristics of people with that negotiation style.

The area in which you scored the highest tends to be the negotiation style that you use the most. Similarly, the area in which you scored the lowest tends to be the negotiation style you use the least.

To learn more about why you tend to use one style more than the others, turn to the next pages for descriptions and exercises for each of the four styles on the scale. Answer all of the questions related to each of the styles.

Analytical People Scale Descriptions

Scale A — Analytical

People with an Analytical Negotiation Style tend to value intelligence and knowledge, and they usually have high standards. They spend a lot of time organizing facts and information in their own minds and are long-range thinkers.

How has being analytical helped you to negotiate for what you wanted? Give an example.

_____

_____

_____

_____

_____

_____

_____

_____

_____

What types of difficulties has being analytical presented when you tried to negotiate? Give an example.

_____

_____

_____

_____

_____

_____

_____

_____

_____

Analytical People – *When Negotiating . . .*

When you negotiate with an expressive person, expect the person to . . .

- display a high level of energy
- show spontaneity
- look at the "big picture" and not the smaller details
- enjoy the process

When you negotiate with an amiable person, expect the person to . . .

- feel before thinking
- focus on aspects other than facts
- attempt to maintain the relationship at all costs
- use intuition rather than logic

When you negotiate with a driven person, expect the person to . . .

- show signs of boredom if you get bogged down in hypothetical situations
- speak his or her mind freely
- strive for results-oriented ideas or solutions
- move at a quick pace

When you negotiate with another analytical person, expect the person to . . .

- provide a logical give-and-take
- organize in detail for the negotiation process
- prepare a lot of facts about the situation
- spend a great deal of time thinking about solutions

How can you now adapt your style when working with people different from you?

_____

_____

_____

_____

_____

_____

_____

Driven People Scale Descriptions

Scale B — Driven

People with a Driven Negotiation Style tend to be born leaders. They are forceful and decisive individuals who make decisions quickly and are quick to verbalize their opinions to the rest of the world. They can have limited patience and are driven to accomplish and bring things to order.

How has being driven helped you to negotiate for what you wanted? Give an example.

_____

_____

_____

_____

_____

_____

_____

_____

_____

What types of difficulties has being driven presented when you tried to negotiate? Give an example.

_____

_____

_____

_____

_____

_____

_____

_____

_____

_____

Driven People – *When Negotiating . . .*

When you negotiate with an expressive person, expect the person to . . .

- show warmth to the other person
- focus on feelings
- be very spontaneous and flexible
- give recognition for his/her contribution

When you negotiate with an amiable person, expect the person to . . .

- slow your pace down so that nothing gets overlooked
- phrase ideas provisionally
- show supportive and empathy
- express interest in the other person's human side

When you negotiate with an analytical person, expect the person to . . .

- listen very carefully and analytically
- be cognizant of the importance of details
- react in a very logical and analytical way to what is being said
- maintain reserve and listen more than talk

When you negotiate with another driven person, expect the person to . . .

- get bored if you get bogged down in hypothetical situations
- speak freely and openly
- be results-oriented
- move at a quick pace

How can you now adapt your style when working with people different from you?

_____

_____

_____

_____

_____

_____

_____

_____

Amiable People Scale Descriptions

Scale – Amiable

People with an Amiable Negotiation Style are warmly interested in other people. For them, developing and maintaining relationships are the most critical aspect of living. They live by certain values and nothing will keep them from expressing those values. They love people and will bring out the best in people.

How has being amiable helped you to negotiate for what you wanted? Give an example.

_____

_____

_____

_____

_____

_____

_____

_____

What types of difficulties has being amiable presented when you tried to negotiate? Give an example.

_____

_____

_____

_____

_____

_____

_____

_____

_____

Amiable People – *When Negotiating . . .*

When you negotiate with an expressive person, expect the person to . . .

- move more quickly than you and get to a solution quickly
- react candidly and directly, and "tell it like it is"
- focus on the big picture, not the details
- use a lot of energy

When negotiating with an analytical person, expect the person to . . .

- attempt to keep people on task, including you
- assert logical conclusions, and not rely on intuition
- emphasize thinking, not feelings
- organize to approach questions and ideas systematically

When negotiating with a driven person, expect the person to . . .

- want to get to the point quickly, maybe too quickly
- expect everyone to be a driven as they are
- identify the task at hand and attempt to find a solution quickly
- express their goals and objectives verbally

When negotiating with another amiable person, expect the person to . . .

- focus on feelings, not thoughts
- focus on other aspects of the negotiation process - not just the facts
- attempt to maintain the relationship at all costs
- prefer intuition to logic

How can you now adapt your style when working with people different from you?

_____

_____

_____

_____

_____

_____

_____

_____

Expressive People Scale Descriptions

Scale D — Expressive

People with an Expressive Negotiation Style live in a world of possibilities. They love people and new experiences, are lively and fun, and do not mind being the center of attention. They live in the here-and-now, and relish excitement and drama in their lives.

How has being expressive helped you to negotiate for what you wanted? Give an example.

_____

_____

_____

_____

_____

_____

_____

_____

_____

_____

What types of difficulties has being expressive presented when you tried to negotiate? Give an example.

_____

_____

_____

_____

_____

_____

_____

_____

_____

_____

_____

Expressive People – *When Negotiating . . .*

When you negotiate with an analytical person, expect the person to . . .

- listen very carefully to what you say and evaluate what is being said
- remain quiet and reserved
- give as much detail as possible — maybe more than you want
- take time to make a decision

When you negotiate with an amiable person, expect the person to . . .

- break the ice with small talk
- try to stop you from rushing through the process
- indicate support and empathy toward people
- be aware of the importance of your relationship, and want to keep it

When you negotiate with a driven person, expect the person to . . .

- display quick actions and direct communications
- attempt to be very forceful in the decision-making process
- indulge in small talk
- emphasize behaviors, not thoughts or feelings

When you negotiate with another expressive person, expect the person to . . .

- maintain a high level of energy
- act with spontaneity
- want the negotiation process to be fun
- look at the "big picture" and not the smaller details

How can you now adapt your style when working with people different from you?

_____

_____

_____

_____

_____

_____

_____

Previous Negotiating Experience Exercise

Negotiation is a process in which individuals come together to resolve their differences and to reach an agreement. In the following spaces, fill in your answers as they relate to times in the past when you have had to negotiate with another person for what you wanted. In the left-hand column, list a previous negotiation situation and in the right-hand column, list what you did to negotiate for what you wanted. These negotiations could be with friends, family members, people at your school, work or community.

PREVIOUS NEGOTIATION SITUATIONS	WHAT I DID TO NEGOTIATE FOR WHAT I WANTED
Negotiating with my partner about which family to spend the holidays with each year.	*I suggested that my partner and I compromise by splitting the trips and we have begun to visit each family every other year.*

Current Negotiating Experience Exercise

Now think about your current situations that need to be negotiated. In the following spaces, fill in your answers as they relate to current situations in which you would like to negotiate with another person for what you want. In the left-hand column, list the current negotiation situation and in the right-hand column, list what you would like to negotiate. These negotiations could be with friends, family members, people at your school, work or community.

CURRENT NEGOTIATION SITUATIONS	WHAT I WOULD LIKE TO NEGOTIATE
I would like to take some college classes, but classes are only offered during the workday. I need to speak with my supervisor.	*I want to negotiate a plan with my supervisor in which I would take a half a day off each week and then make up the time on the weekend or stay late several evenings.*

The Negotiation Process

When you find yourself negotiating with another person for something you desire, consider some specific steps you can take to ensure a mutually-beneficial outcome.

Step 1 – Maintain a positive attitude

- Attitude is critical in most negotiations
- Remember that everything is negotiable
- Have patience to find a solution
- Maintain an attitude of honesty and integrity
- Assume that you will compromise
- Understand the other person's negotiating style

Step 2 – Communicate effectively

- Establish rapport based on mutual interests
- Remember that fairness elicits fairness in return
- Know that generosity leads to generosity
- Try to put yourself in the other person's shoes
- Be cooperative, but don't let your guard down

Step 3 – Develop a plan for what you want

- Plan your initial offer carefully
- Don't give too much away too early
- Try to achieve your goals, but plan to make concessions

Step 4 – Look for multiple solutions

- Explore options – there is not only one solution

Step 5 – Come to closure

- Try to do what you can to maintain the relationship
- Bring the negotiation to closure
- Don't forget about emotional closure with the other person / people

Practicing the Negotiation Process

When you find yourself negotiating with another person for something you desire, practice the specific steps you learned to ensure a mutually-beneficial outcome. Think about a current situation you listed that needs to be negotiated.

List it: _____

Step 1 – Maintain a positive attitude (have patience, be honest)

What are you willing to compromise? _____

What is the other person's negotiating style? _____

Step 2 – Communicate effectively (consider the other person's point of view, cooperate)

Establish rapport: What are your mutual interests? _____

Be fair and generous: What are you willing to give up? _____

_____

_____

Step 3 – Develop a plan for what you want (Don't give away too much)

What will be your initial offer? _____

_____

_____

What are your goals? _____

_____

_____

Step 4 – Look for multiple solutions (maintain the relationship)

Brainstorm options: _____

_____

_____

Step 5 – Come to closure

How will you develop emotional closure with the person? _____

_____

_____

Strengths and Weaknesses
of My Negotiation Style

What would you say are the strengths of your negotiation style?

_____

_____

_____

_____

_____

_____

_____

_____

_____

_____

_____

_____

_____

What would you say are the weaknesses of your negotiation style?

_____

_____

_____

_____

_____

_____

_____

_____

_____

_____

_____

_____

_____

I Have Learned . . .

What did you learn about yourself that can help you in negotiating?

_____
_____
_____
_____
_____
_____
_____
_____
_____
_____
_____
_____

What did you learn about other people that can help you in negotiating?

_____
_____
_____
_____
_____
_____
_____
_____
_____
_____
_____
_____

Tips for Brainstorming Solutions

When brainstorming solutions in the negotiation process, support yourself with these tips . . .

- Develop a large list of ideas

- The more ideas you generate, the better

- No ideas are "bad" ideas

- Criticism is not allowed

- Ideas should not be attributed to the person who suggested them

- Rank order solutions from best to worst

- Always look for *win-win* solutions

Information about Conflict

- Conflict is inevitable

- Conflict happens at home, work, school and in the community

- Conflict can be avoided, minimized or diverted

- Signs of an impending conflict are recognizable

- Strategies to resolve conflicts effectively can be learned

wholeperson

Whole Person Associates is the leading publisher of training resources for professionals who empower people to create and maintain healthy lifestyles. Our creative resources will help you work effectively with your clients in the areas of stress management, wellness promotion, mental health and life skills.

Please visit us at our web site: **www.wholeperson.com**. You can check out our entire line of products, place an order, request our print catalog, and sign up for our monthly special notifications.

Whole Person Associates

800-247-6789

© 2010 WHOLE PERSON ASSOCIATES, 101 W. 2ND ST., SUITE 203, DULUTH MN 55802 ▪ 800-247-6789